The Perfecting

of

the Saints

Coming Forth as Gold

By

Allan Smith

Pastor, New World Christian Center

The Perfecting of the Saints: Coming Forth As Gold
By Allan Smith

This book or any parts of it may not be reproduced in any form without prior permission of the author.

Unless otherwise indicated, all scripture passages quoted are from the King James Version of the Bible.

ISBN   1453668578

Copyright © 2010 by Allan Smith

www.newworldcc.org

Printed in the United States of America

2010 – First Edition

Contents

Introduction	5
1 The Kingdom of God Must Be Your Goal	8
2 Job as an Example of Perfection	13
3 Methods that Satan May Use to Test Your Perfection	21
4 You Must Be Equipped to Withstand Satan's Attack	31
5 Satan's Use of Traditions, Rituals, or False Doctrines	39
6 You Must Not Complain	55
7 Strategies to Use in Times of Difficulties	66
8 How to Achieve Perfection	75
9 Scriptural References to Perfection	85

Ephesians 4:11 – 12: *"And he gave some, apostles; and some, prophets; and some, evangelists; and some, pastors and teachers; 12)* <u>*for the perfecting of the saints*</u>*, for the work of the ministry, for the edifying of the body of Christ: 13) Till we all come in the unity of the faith, and of the knowledge of the Son of God, unto a perfect man, unto the measure of the stature of the fulness of Christ: 14) That we henceforth be no more children, tossed to and fro, and carried about with every wind of doctrine, by the sleight of men, and cunning craftiness, whereby they lie in wait to deceive;… 15) But speaking the truth in love, may grow up into him in all things, which is the head, even Christ:*

Introduction

Job 23:10-12: *But he knoweth the way that I take: when he hath tried me, I shall come forth as gold. 11) My foot hath held his steps, his way have I kept, and not declined. 12) Neither have I gone back from the commandment of his lips; I have esteemed the words of his mouth more than my necessary food.*

Now that is perfection! And God bragged on Job about how he was perfect, and upright, and feared God, and eschewed evil.

As Christians, you *must* aim for perfection in the Kingdom of God. You must be mindful of what Jesus says in Matthew 5:48, *"Be ye therefore perfect, even as your Father which is in heaven is perfect."* You must be perfected in the things of God. You must diligently seek wisdom in the things of God. Perfection must be your never ending goal, and you must work at it daily until it is achieved. Perfection requires that you live a God-fearing life, putting first the things concerning the Kingdom of God. Perfection takes place on the inside and manifests itself on the outside. This "inside perfection", so to speak, cannot be perceived by others, but can be observed by your actions and attitudes to others – that is, the "outside perfection". So the outside perfection is dependent on the inside perfection. Just so, imperfection (evil thoughts) takes place on the inside and manifests itself on the outside (evil words and actions).

Matthew 15:11, 18-20: *"Not that which goeth into the mouth defileth a man; but that which cometh out of the mouth, this defileth a man.... 18) But those things which proceed out of the mouth come forth from the heart; and they defile* (makes him imperfect) *the man. 19) For out of the heart proceed evil thoughts, murders, adulteries, fornications, thefts, false witness, blasphemies: 20) These are the things which defile a man: but to eat with unwashen hands defileth not a man."* Proverbs 23:7 says, *"For as he thinketh in his heart, so is he:...."*

1

The Kingdom of God Must Be Your Goal

Your goal in seeking perfection is to have the kingdom of God in your hearts. Your everyday life must reflect what is in your hearts. You must strive for your very existence to be Christ-like. That is the only way. There is no other way. Any other way is imperfection

1. You must be willing to accept the teachings of the gospel as the true and only word of God. Romans 8:14-15: *"For as many as are led by the Spirit of God, they are the sons of God."*

2. Be prepared to follow diligently, without wavering, the word of God. Philippians 3:12-21: *"Not as though I had already attained,*

either were already perfect: but I follow after, if that I may apprehend that for which also I am apprehended of Christ Jesus."

3. Through the knowledge of God's word you will be able to withstand the Devil. In Mathew chapter 4 is shown how Jesus was able to rebuff the temptations of the Devil by using the written word of God. Matthew 4:*4: "But he* [Jesus] *answered and said, It is written, Man shall not live by bread alone,* (imperfection) *but by every word that proceedeth out of the mouth of God.* (perfection). (Also see Job 1:1).

4. Know that Satan will have you focusing on material things, but God wants you to focus on spiritual things. In Matthew 6:33 Jesus states, *"But seek ye first the kingdom of God, and his righteousness; and all these things shall be added unto you."*

5. You must be able to withstand criticisms and put downs, and insults. Certain people are going to come in your life to attempt to ridicule you. Know that these are messengers from Satan. Be careful. You will see later in this book how Job's three friends sought to ridicule and accuse him of being a hypocrite. In Job 4:1-11, his friend Eliphaz declares he (job) has sinned.

I used Job in this discussion to enlighten you on what is perfection. Perfection, therefore, can withstand any assault by Satan and his forces, since it relies on the Holy Spirit, that is in you. To be perfect means to live your life in obedience to the Word of God. With the power of the Holy Spirit in you, you are able to prosper in all areas of your life. You are able to be perfect, "… as your Father … in heaven.…"

So the saints, and that means you, become perfected through experiencing all types of trials, tribulations, and temptations and surviving spiritually intact because of your trust in God.

Who are the saints you may ask? All who have given their lives over to God through Jesus Christ. Observe what Romans 1:7 says, *"To all that be in Rome, beloved of God, called* to be *saints."* Romans 15:25 states, *"But now I go unto Jerusalem to minister unto the saints."* Saints means the Christians at who lived in Rome at that time. Amen.

Notes

2

Job as an Example of Perfection

This brings us to Job. (See Job 1:1). Job was a "perfectionist" in obeying the word of God. Not only was he blessed materially, but also spiritually. That is perfection. This is the kind of perfection that the saints of God must seek. Observe how God himself describes Job to Satan: Job 1:8: *"And the LORD said unto Satan, Hast thou considered my servant Job, that there is none like him in the earth, a perfect and an upright man, one that feareth God, and escheweth evil?"* God describes Job among other things as perfect. God is perfection. He knows perfection. So if He says Job is perfect, then Job must have been perfect.

Things to note as you read further in this book:

- Satan is throwing everything at Job.
- Satan is attempting to destroy perfection.
- Satan is trying to prove Job a hypocrite.
- Satan is trying to prove that perfection is in material things.
- Perfection must be able to withstand criticism.
- Perfection must be able to withstand false accusations.
- Perfection must be able to withstand mockery.

Why am I focusing on Job? Because God said he was perfect. Therefore he must be a good example for all Christians to follow. And if Job is truly perfect then he must be able to survive all that Satan throws at him. Now see what happens. Note again

Matthew 5:48 states, *"Be ye perfect even as my Father in heaven is perfect."* So God is perfect and knows perfection. If God says Job is perfect then job must be perfect. So Job is a "perfect" example of perfection. Who said Job was perfect? God did. Is God qualified to say Job was perfect? Of course. The question is, What makes Job perfect? What did God see about Job? God saw Job's spiritual lifestyle.

In addition to Job's impeccable spiritual lifestyle, he is also very, very rich. Job 1:2, 3 state, *"And there were born unto him seven sons and three daughters. 3) His substance also was seven thousand sheep, and three thousand camels, and five hundred yoke of oxen, and five hundred she asses, and a very great household; so that this man was the greatest of all the men of the east."*

What have you noticed about job so far? He is spiritually rich and materially rich. One thing for sure is that Job did not factor Satan in the equation of his life. All with him was perfect. Everything he planned so far was realized. All his dreams have come true. He is living the good life, the abundant life. He is the greatest of all men in the east. He has a great household, servants, and vast possessions, a wife and ten children.

In Job 1:8 we see God bragging on Job to Satan: *"And the LORD said unto Satan, 'Hast thou considered my servant Job, that there is none like him in the earth, a perfect and an upright man, one that feareth God, and escheweth evil?'"* Observe Satan's reply to God in Job 1:9-*10, "Then Satan answered the LORD, and said, 'Doth Job fear God for naught? 10) Hast not thou made a hedge about him, and about his house, and about all that he hath on every side? thou hast blessed the work of his hands, and his substance is increased in the land'."*

Do you see the difference between God's focus and Satan's? God is focusing on the spiritual, whereas Satan is focusing on the material. While God equates spiritual completeness with perfection,

Satan equates material success with perfection; this is how you, the saints, get defeated. Satan has you thinking that if you have achieve worldly success – great jobs, big houses, fancy cars, etc., you have made it. You are now perfect, but God wants you to focus on spiritual things. That is why God highlighted Job's spiritual nature. God was certain that because of Job's spiritual strength, he (Job) would remain perfect even if he loses all his material goods.

As I said before God is perfect, and understands what it takes to be perfect, and knew that Job had perfection in him, through the Holy Spirit. Satan on the other hand is trying to prove Job is a hypocrite, and that he (Job) is not all that spiritually strong as God says he is, but that Job is pretending because God has blessed him with all those material things. After all, Job "was the greatest of all the men of the east", and a very successful business man just like any of the world's richest men. What set Job apart was the he was not only materially rich, but more importantly, he was spiritually rich. And that is what makes the difference between your victory or defeat.

So Satan attempts to trick you by keeping your minds focused on accumulating material things. That is the way of the world. People tend to see you as successful, and that your life is perfect if they see you with lots of material possessions, but think you are a loser if your spiritual life outweighs your material life. That is why Jesus said in Matthew 6:19-21, *"Lay not up for yourselves treasures upon earth, where moth and rust doth corrupt, and where thieves break through and steal: 20) But lay up for yourselves treasures in heaven, where neither moth nor rust doth corrupt, and where thieves do not break through nor steal: 21) For where your treasure is, there will your heart be also."* Jesus is sounding a warning to you to be aware of the dangers of seeing your material possessions as your treasure. On the contrary, you should only treasure spiritual things. This brings perfection.

You are to lay up treasures in heaven, for where your treasure is, there is your heart also. When you focus on earthly things, you lose that relationship with God, that relationship you will need when the storms come into your life. Job was able to face down the storm because of his faith in God, because he did not live by his possessions alone, but by every word of God. God said Job was perfect…. God bragged on Job. Job had attained perfection, and could not be shaken by Satan. Just as Jesus' test in the wilderness was a test of his perfection. Job never once considered denying God.

Notes

3

Methods that Satan May Use to Test Your Perfection

Satan is determined to test you to prove you are not as perfect as you think, to see how strong your faith is in God. Observe how he uses Job's friends in an attempt to throw him (Job) off track.

I now come to the point where Job's friends having heard of his illness came to visit him. Of the three friends, Eliphaz is the first to speak. In Job chapter 4, Eliphaz begins by admonishing Job. Observe Job 4:1-9: *"Then Eliphaz the Temanite answered and said, 2) If we attempt to commune with thee, wilt thou be grieved? but who can withhold himself from speaking? 3) Behold, thou hast instructed many, and thou hast strengthened the weak hands. 4) Thy words have upheld him that was falling, and thou hast strengthened the feeble knees. 5) But now it is come upon thee, and thou faintest; it toucheth thee, and thou art troubled. 6) Is not this thy fear, thy confidence, thy hope, and the uprightness of thy ways? 7) Remember, I pray thee, who ever perished, being innocent? or where were the righteous cut off? 8) Even as I have seen, they that plow iniquity, and sow wickedness, reap the same. 9) By the blast of God they perish, and by the breath of his nostrils are they consumed."*

Eliphaz is saying to Job you have instructed, comforted, and counseled people who were in the same situation as you are now. How come you cannot deal with your situation? You ought to be able to handle it. You ought to be strong because you have all the answers. Look at verse 5 of Job chapter 4: *"But now it is come upon thee, and thou faintest; it toucheth thee, and thou art troubled."* Eliphaz is saying to Job, you of all people should not be troubled. You of all people should not "faint". You of all people should be able to stand in the midst of all this with a smile on your face. You, Job, must be a hypocrite! You never believed in what you said in the first place.

The question you must be asking is, What kind of friend is Eliphaz? Do you need a friend like him? And, as if questioning Job's integrity was not enough, he continues his relentless rant by suggesting that God always punishes the guilty, and the unrighteous. Observe verses 7 through 9 above. He mercilessly lays into the suffering Job by telling him that the innocent never perishes, the righteous are never cut off from God, and those who sow evil reap evil. How is that for support? How is that for compassion? How is that for comfort? How is that for testing your perfection?

A friend who comes to you in time of your need must show compassion, kindness and love, not add to your troubles by chastising and criticizing you. None of Job's friends brought him any comforting words. It was all condemnation, criticism. In his time of need they should have shown compassion, love, kindness.

Perfection depends heavily on the knowledge of how God works (Job had that knowledge. Not only was Job patient, but was also wise spiritually and in business).

When your friends approach you as Job's friends did, you must know that they are messengers of Satan. Be prepared to rebuke them with the word of God. That is where the shield of faith and the sword of the spirit come into play. This what Jesus did in the wilderness- (Mathew Chapter 4). This what Job did in chapter 12 of the Book of Job.

But all this attack on Job is by design. It is a planned strategy of Satan to use Job's friends to turn him against God, to prove that he is not perfect as God says. Eliphaz is presenting false doctrine to Job.

That is why as Christians you must be aware of those who come to you mouthing what appears to be the word of God, but is nothing but the twisted doctrine of a mind controlled by Satan. In this context, knowledge of the word of God is essential to keeping you firm footed, for you to be able to stand.

Satan has progressed from destroying Job's property and children, to attacking him physically, but he could not shake Job's faith in God. Now he turns to the battle in the mind.

Observe Job 1:22: *"In all this Job sinned not, nor charged God foolishly."* That statement speaks of perfection, and uprightness, fear of God, and shunning of evil. Remember, the battle for your spiritual well-being takes place in the mind. You must have heard the old saying that "an idle mind is the Devil's workshop." That may be the case, but more importantly, for Christians, is that a mind that is lacking God's truths is open to suggestions and control by the Devil. Such a mind presents a ready battlefield with the advantage in Satan's favor, and a swift and decisive victory for the forces of evil.

Satan's intent for Job was to overcome him, to conquer him, to turn him against God and draw him into his camp. The taking away of Job's material things was the beginning of the battle in the mind. That was stage one in Satan's strategy. It just did not work with Job. So Satan moved on to stage two by attempting to use his (Job's) wife against him. Observe this: Job 2:9 states, *"Then said his wife unto him, Dost thou still retain thine integrity? curse God, and die."* How is that for wifely advice? How is that for spiritual guidance? These are the words of Satan himself spoken by Job's wife. Satan will stop at nothing to destroy you, the saints of God. He will use your own family members against you, if he thinks he has the smallest chance of defeating you, to prove you are not perfect in Christ.

Now he turns to using Job's three friends in a lengthy and relentless mind game in an attempt to conquer Job's spirit and to prove to God that Job is not "all that". On to stage three! Throughout the discussion, the main theme of Job's friends was that Job was a hypocrite, a pretender, a man who must have sinned against God at some point in his life, and who is now paying for it at the hand of God. It was a vicious assault on Job, especially given the shaky mental state in which Job was. It was as if Job was at the edge of a cliff and Satan, through Job's friends, was attempting to give him that final push over the edge. Satan shows no mercy to his intended victims. His only intention is "to steal, to kill, and to destroy" by any means necessary. For him it is victory no matter what. There is no reasoning with him. You must be prepared. You must be spiritually perfect, or else!

The questions I am asking here are, Are you equipped to handle Satan's attacks? Can you survive stage one? If Satan takes away you material possessions, what is going to be your reaction as children and saints of God? If Satan follows this with an attack of sickness like he did Job, are you prepared to handle this or are you going to take Job's wife's advice and "curse God and die?" How about stage three with Job's friends? Do you have friends like those who are ready to criticize and bury you with all kinds of Bible misquotes? How do you handle those friends? How steady is your mind? Is your mind set on a firm foundation? Are you wearing the armor of God, or is it sitting locked away in a closet somewhere at the back of your mind? Are you ready to wield the sword of the spirit (the word of God as told in the Bible) when your friends confront you and call you a hypocrite, or is it gathering dust in the top shelf of your dusty closet? These are the questions I want you consider. Think hard on these things, and see where you stand. Be honest with whomever you discuss this message. Colossians 3:16 states, *"Let the word of Christ dwell in you richly in all wisdom; teaching and admonishing one another in psalms and hymns spiritual songs, singing with grace in your hearts to the Lord."*

Did you think about those questions posed above? If you did, I hope you were honest to yourselves in your answers, and that you found enlightenment in them. Remember, spiritual perfection depends not only on your knowledge of how God works, but having strong faith in God.

Notes

4

You Must Be Equipped to Withstand Satan's Attack

Now let us take a look at some likely responses to those questions asked. Are you equipped to handle Satan's attacks? Let us see how Job responded. Job 1:22 *"In all this Job sinned not, nor charged God foolishly."* Notice, Job did not turn to sin in response to his devastating situation. I have known some people to turn away from God when they face trials. A young lady once remarked to me that she no longer goes to church because her brother died when he was fourteen years old and she could not handle the fact that "God let him die so young." Another young man at whose house we gathered once a week for Bible study said he no longer believed in God because of an unexpected unfortunate incident in his life. Do you know anyone like those two? They lacked perfection! Pray for them! This was indeed a victory for Satan. This was the response Satan hoped he would hear from Job. You saw how Job responded to his wife's suggestion "to curse God and die." At this point you should have had a discussion with your spouse or family members. How strong is your spouse's or family members' faith? What advice or support will they give you in your time of distress? Believe me, this is important. This is the time to assist each other in building up each other's faith through prayer and knowledge of God's word. Remember, "faith comes by hearing, and what is heard is the word of God." You do not want that weak-link spouse or family member to influence you to take ungodly steps. Most importantly *you* have to be strong in the Lord so you can rebuke Satan when he comes at you through your spouse or other family member.

Now (not today nor tomorrow nor next week) is the appropriate time to prepare to deal with those otherwise "good" Christian friends of yours who quote from the Bible at the drop of a hat. You know, those who have a list of what gets you into hell. There is no need to get upset with them. Just stay focused on the word, standing firm-footed in the gospel of peace, wearing that armor of God, ministering to them if need be so all of you will benefit. Call them over and have Bible study, so all can be on the path to perfection. Observe: Hebrew 3:13 states, *"But exhort one another daily, while it is called Today; lest any of you be hardened through the deceitfulness of sin,"* and Colossians 3:16, *"Let the word of Christ dwell in you richly in all wisdom; teaching and admonishing one another in psalms and hymns and spiritual songs, singing with grace in your hearts to the Lord."* This will protect you in times when it seems as though you are walking through the valley of the shadow of death. Remember David's words in Psalm 23:4, *"Yea, though I walk through the valley of the shadow of death, I will fear no evil: for thou art with me; thy rod and thy staff they comfort me."* The point is get to your "Christian" friends before they get to you and mislead you. This not only strengthens your mind, but builds up your confidence in God.

Job was able to handle his friends because he was anchored in the word of God. Something held him back from falling into the abyss of sin against God. As his friends pummeled him with misquotes and name calling he never crossed the line into Satan's kingdom. Though he moaned and whined and was physically hurt, he was strong enough in the spirit to stand! Great spiritual strength can overcome even greater physical harm.

Yes, at times Job seemed as though he was on the brink of losing his mind. He complained and whined bitterly, and appeared to be getting closer and closer to that door of no return, but in the end he held firm. He was perfect! Matthew 5:48 *"Be ye therefore perfect, even as your Father which is in heaven is perfect."*

Now, let us recall some things that you need to be aware of as you move forward along the path to perfection. Perfection must be able to withstand criticism. Perfection will be able to withstand false accusations. Perfection will be able to withstand all types of temptations to go against God's will, or to put it plainly, to do wrong in the sight of God. Perfection will be able to discern and resist false doctrine. You must be aware of friends, family, spouses, close associates giving you false doctrine. You run the risk of falling into Satan's trap. Be careful of traditions and rituals.

You may remember from reading the book of Job how Job's friends, Eliphaz, Bildad, and Zophar, criticized him during his time of grief and suffering. They acted like messengers of Satan attempting to put doubt in Job's mind. Here is what Eliphaz had to say in Job 4:7, *"Remember, I pray thee, who ever perished, being innocent? or where were the righteous cut off?"* Eliphaz is saying to Job you must have done something evil. That is why you are being punished by God. Here is what Bildad had to say in Job 8:6: *"If thou wast pure and upright; surely now he* [God] *would awake for thee, and make the habitation of thy righteousness prosperous."* Zophar shows no mercy in Job 11:3: *"Should thy lies make men hold their peace? and when thou mockest, shall no man make thee ashamed?"* and Job 11:5 states, *"But oh that God would speak, and open his lips against thee."*

Will you able to withstand a vicious attack like that? How will you respond if your best friends approach you when you are most stressed out from a troubling situation with that kind of attack? How would you respond if your own family whom you trust is trying to commit an evil plot against you? What will you honestly say to them? Will you keep your cool? Knowing who you are, will you let it slide? Will you maintain "your integrity"? Come on now, be honest. Look at the man/woman in the mirror as you attempt to answer these questions. Do you think you may need to change your ways? Think about a bad, past experience. How did you respond to that situation? How would you respond now? Will you stand your spiritual ground? Will you be perfect?

Notes

5

Satan's Use of Traditions, Rituals, or False Doctrines

How about false doctrine, you know those misquotes you have heard all your life? In effect that is what Job's friends were doing. They were saying to him words that you and I have heard all our lives. "God is going to whip you!" How untrue!!! They were actually telling Job that God punished him for something wrong that he did, and that was far from the truth. Satan afflicted Job, not God!!! What false doctrine! You may have heard this before. This may have stemmed in part from the fact of what is written in Job 1:20, 21: *"Then Job arose, and rent his mantle, and shaved his head, and fell down upon the ground, and worshipped, 21) And said, Naked came I out of my mother's womb, and naked shall I return thither: the LORD gave, and the LORD hath taken away; blessed be the name of the LORD."* But God took nothing from Job, Satan did!

You must be aware of false doctrine. It leaves you with no legs to stand on when the thief comes, to steal, to kill and to destroy.

Observe these passages of scripture in Matthew 24:11: *"And many false prophets shall rise, and shall deceive many."* In Mark 13:22: *"For false Christs and false prophets shall rise, and shall show signs and wonders, to seduce, if it were possible, even the elect."* In 2 Corinthians 11:13: *"For such are false apostles, deceitful workers, transforming themselves into the apostles of Christ."* In 1 John 4:1: *"Beloved, believe not every spirit, but try the spirits whether they are of God: because many false prophets are gone out into the world."*

False doctrine is designed by Satan to lead you away from God and the path to perfection. The intent is to leave you defenseless, so when trials and problems come your way you do not have the true word of God to stand on. You can then be easily defeated. The problem of false doctrine has its roots in churches that have strayed from the true word of God, and have shifted their focus on meaningless rituals in order to please the congregation before them, and keep their membership up. This is a clever trick of Satan to keep you and the body of Christ ignorant of the word of God, and from perfection.

Are you able to recognize false doctrine? Ask yourself the question, Have I ever followed, or am I following, false doctrine? Are there some things I need to change? Think on these things.

I now turn to traditions and rituals that are the chief result of false doctrine. Just as we saw Job's three friends telling him falsely about how God works, we find today certain preachers and teachers of the "word" speak doctrine that is not lined up with the word of God.

Many of the prosperity preachers are particularly guilty of this. You may have heard some speak of first fruits, admonishing Christians in their congregation and on television that they will be financially blessed if they give the first fruits of their labor. Some even take it a step further to say that you must give your first pay check of the year to them (well, to the church) and you will receive a great financial return. But is that the whole truth? I submit to you it is far from the whole truth, and if not the whole truth, then it constitutes false doctrine. Some preachers stress the importance of tithing, and that is good. Tithing is necessary for the upkeep of the church and helping in financing the spreading of God's word, but when tithing is linked to financial return that makes it false doctrine. And not only that, but by linking tithing with the expectation of a financial windfall on the giver's part, creates in the tither a mindset that he/she is making an financial investment. What happens when the "financial blessing" does not materialize? There is a chance that the tither becomes frustrated, and when this happens we have someone who loses faith in Christianity. When false hope is promoted, it leads to disillusionment, and then, to lost souls. The focus should be on giving with a willing heart. False doctrine is of Satan, meant to destroy the Kingdom of God.

Observe in Malachi 3:10: *"Bring ye all the tithes into the storehouse, that there may be meat in mine house, and prove me now herewith, saith the LORD of hosts, if I will not open you the windows of heaven, and pour you out a blessing, that there shall not be room enough to receive it".* Your primary concern is to bring the tithes, and the blessing will follow. Whether it is financial blessing or not, is not spelled out in God's promise. Therefore the blessing may take any form, and with the blessing, others (the poor, the less fortunate) will be blessed by you giving to their comfort.

Now let me turn to first fruits. Proverbs 3:9 " *Honour the LORD with thy substance, and with the firstfruits of all thine increase: 10) So shall thy barns be filled with plenty, and thy presses shall burst out with new wine."* The focus must be on honoring the Lord, not on what you will receive if you honor the Lord. Filled barns and bursting presses, in other words, abundance, are not a return on an investment, but a blessing from God because of your generous giving from a righteous heart.

So far we have seen that tithing and giving of first fruits are followed by promises of abundance from God, but that only half of the truth, and this is the half that the masters of false doctrine hang on to and preach. So what is the other half that completes the whole truth? Matthew 6:33 states clearly, *"But seek ye first the kingdom of God, and his righteousness; and all these things shall be added unto you."* The other half, then, constitutes seeking the kingdom, so when you give you do so out of a righteous heart, and not on the thought of expecting a windfall financial blessing in return. When your focus is on financial returns, then your heart will be on finances (money), and not on God. As Jesus stated in Matthew 6:21 *"For where your treasure is, there will your heart be also."* As Paul so eloquently puts it in 1 Corinthians 13:3, *"And though I bestow all my goods to feed the poor, and though I give my body to be burned, and have not charity (love), it profiteth me nothing."* Therein lies the other half of the whole. So continue to give generously, with love in your hearts, not as an investment with your focus on a financial windfall, but as a gift to the furtherance of the kingdom of God.

Let me say this clearly, that traditions and rituals do not in themselves pose any harm to Christian worship. The problem arises when these traditions become the focus of worship, or what is worshipped. For example, there are those who are more caught up with the order of worship than the worship itself. This leads to bickering, divisions and strife in the church, because there would be some who think that the offering should be taken before the announcements are made, while others may think that the announcements should be at the end of the pastor's sermon. These trifle matters can sometimes get out of hand and cause immeasurable damage to harmony in the church.

Observe this: Paul is writing to the Corinthian Christians in 1 Corinthians 1:10, *"Now I beseech you, brethren, by the name of our Lord Jesus Christ, that ye all speak the same thing, and that there be no divisions among you; but that ye be perfectly joined together in the same mind and in the same judgment."* That is in the same mind and the same judgment based on God's word and not man's invention. The focus in every church *must* be the word of God and nothing else. If you attend a church where the focus is on baseless traditions, it is time the rethink your situation. Remember this: John 15:14 states, *"Ye are my friends, if ye do whatsoever I command you."* You must do what Jesus says and not follow traditions that get you nowhere.

We find all kinds of traditions, such as there should be a "devotion" time before worship starts. And what about the belief that women should not wear pants? I have seen people go into a fit when women enter the church in pants. One staunch "traditionalist" thought it outrageous when a female visitor to her church took a seat at the platform with the other ministers while she (the female visitor) was dressed in a pants suit. I mean this "traditionalist" was almost frothing at the mouth. What does the Bible say about this? Deuteronomy 22:5 states, *"The woman shall not wear that which pertaineth unto a man, neither shall a man put on a woman's garment: for all that do so are abomination unto the LORD thy God."* Notice the passage does not say anything about women and pants. On the contrary it says, to paraphrase, men's clothing and women's clothing. The point is, there are men's pants – pants designed for men, and also women's pants – pants designed for women. Just so there are hats designed for men and hats designed for women. But no matter which way you look at it, how does clothing affect your relationship with Christ? Keep the focus folks!

Then, there is a certain Christian church denomination which encourages its members to pray to Holy Mary mother of God. Now is that found in the scripture? And are the rosary and the confession booth? From where did these rituals come? Can you answer those questions? Then there are those who are taught by some preachers to do the "ritual" of the "Daniel Fast"? And some believe that by doing the "fast" without even changing their lifestyle they would get the benefit of prosperity. Is that Biblical? How misleading and dishonest! Ask yourself the question, "Why did Daniel fast?" (See Daniel Ch 10). And in your finding out, you will discover what kind of man Daniel was. Are you getting the picture?

The bottom line is, you have to get your focus off these "traditions and rituals" and put it on the Word. Many people love those traditions because it makes them feel free to do whatever they want to do without the feeling of guilt. Churches today are packed with these "Christians". Not to say that any of you who are receiving this message falls in that group.

Observe Jesus inMatthew 23:23: *"Woe unto you, scribes and Pharisees, hypocrites! for ye pay tithe of mint and anise and cummin, and have omitted the weightier matters of the law, judgment, mercy, and faith: these ought ye to have done, and not to leave the other undone."*

In the above passage, Jesus is critical of the scribes and Pharisees because their focus is on tithing and how much tithe is being paid and not on having their hearts lined up with the word of God. The point here is, what benefit is it to you for paying your tithes if your heart is not right? Again, with reference to Paul as he explains in 1 Corinthians 13:3: *"And though I bestow all my goods to feed the poor, and though I give my body to be burned, and have not charity (love in our hearts for others), it profiteth me nothing".* Now, I am not saying, do not pay your tithes. God commanded us to do so, but have love also in your heart, as Jesus puts it, the "weightier matters of the Law. You see if you have love, paying your tithes becomes easy.

Now what about talking in tongues? Certain churches believe in this. Actually, there is a particular Christian denomination that believes this and practices "speaking in tongues" as an integral part of their worship service. But is this Biblical? The short answer is no! Again, practicing this ritual gains you nothing, especially when you make it an end in itself. When you enter a church and the entire congregation appears to be "speaking in tongues", but on closer listening it amounts to nothing more than untranslatable babbling, then something is Biblically wrong. Why is it necessary for a group of people in a congregation where all speak the same language, say English, just suddenly start "speaking in tongues" – another language or languages? Do you see the picture? Now, observe this. Paul to the Corinthians: 1 Corinthians 14:23 *"If therefore the whole church be come together into one place, and all speak with tongues, and there come in those that are unlearned, or unbelievers, will they not say that ye are mad?"* 1 Corinthians 13:1 states: *"Though I speak with the tongues of men and of angels, and have not charity (love), I am become as sounding brass, or a tinkling cymbal."*

The point is that you must able to discern "traditions, rituals, and false doctrines" and avoid them. Let your focus be only on God's word. Relying on false doctrine will deny you perfection in the Kingdom. John 13:34 states, *"A new commandment I give unto you, That ye love one another; as I have loved you, that ye also love one another."* This commandment replaces all the other commandments, and frees you from all those "traditions." As one famous preacher puts it, this commandment constitutes "an amendment to the constitution of Heaven."

The point is that these traditions, rituals, and false doctrines are designed by Satan to draw you away from God, thereby proving that you are not perfect. Perfection comes through the knowledge of God's Word, and knowledge of God's Word gives insight into how God works, which in turn will allows you to be able to discern false doctrine, so your spiritual perfection cannot be shaken. In this case, perfection is demonstrated by your realization and nonparticipation in those activities that are contrary to the will of God.

Notes

6

You Must Not Complain

As Christians you must be aware that when you are faced with trials, tribulations, or unfortunate situations you must not turn to complaining, or feeling sorry for yourself. Complaining can lead you to a misinterpretation of God's plans for your life, which in turn can lead you to lose your trust and faith in God. You then make the wrong decisions about your life, complicating matters and making your already "bad" situation worse. I put "bad" in quotations because if you look at your situation from God's perspective it is not really "bad". The truth is that God sometimes allow Satan to bring "bad" experiences in your life to lead you to a higher level of faith. When you begin to complain and you get into the "why me" mode you lose the focus on God, and you can now be easily influenced by friends and family acting on behalf of Satan (even though they may not know it) who will give you the wrong advice. Remember Job's wife's advice to him in Job 2:9: *"Then said his wife unto him, 'Dost thou still retain thine integrity? Curse God, and die'."* What if Job had not trusted in God? What if in his complaining he had gone over the edge? Do you see the danger here? Is your faith as strong as Job's where you can get to the edge of that cliff of disaster and not fall into the abyss of sin? This is what Satan wants. He wants you destroyed. And the only way he can do so is to have you turn away from God. Complaining can lead to that. Complaining or feeling sorry for yourself can lead you to focus on the problem to the point where you no longer focus on God. You tend to put off you relationship with God as you wait for the problem to be fixed. This is where Satan wants you, because as long as you stop fully focusing on God, the problem remains, and you are defeated. You have become sidetracked and are no longer on the road to perfection. Unbridled complaining, therefore, is like an exit sign on the path to perfection.

Observe a small sample of Job's complaint. Job 3:1-6, 11 states, *"After this opened Job his mouth, and cursed his day. 2) And Job spake, and said, 3) Let the day perish wherein I was born, and the night in which it was said, There is a man child conceived. 4) Let that day be darkness; let not God regard it from above, neither let the light shine upon it. 5) Let darkness and the shadow of death stain it; let a cloud dwell upon it; let the blackness of the day terrify it. 6) As for that night, let darkness seize upon it; let it not be joined unto the days of the year, let it not come into the number of the months.... 11) Why died I not from the womb? why did I not give up the ghost when I came out of the belly?"*

The question for you is, Can you get to this distressed state when faced with unfortunate situations and maintain your trust in God? To not do so is fraught with danger. Do you see the extent to which Job has taken his complaint? It borders on bitterness. He is standing on the edge of disaster, in deep despair. Now, your assignment is to read Job chapter 3 and get an insight into Job's state of mind. Then look yourself in the mirror and ask yourself the question, "Do you (self) really, really want to go there?" Will I be able to recover from there? Now, let us see what the Bible says about complaining. Paul writes to the Philippian Christians: Philippians 4: 6-*7 states, "Be anxious for nothing, but in everything by prayer and supplication, with thanksgiving, let your requests be made known to God; 7) and the peace of God, which surpasses all understanding, will guard your hearts and minds through Christ Jesus."* NKJV. Paul is saying, no need to get frustrated, no need to get angry, no need for despair, or to be stressed out, no need for sleepless nights and midnight "pity parties". Being overcome with anxiety could lead you away from God. Just pray and trust.

Observe 1 Corinthians 10:10: *"And do not grumble, as some of them did—and were killed by the destroying angel."* Psalm 106:25 states, *"They grumbled in their tents and did not obey the LORD."* For most of the book of Job, Job complained bitterly about the unfair treatment he thinks he is getting at the hands of God. In one of the greatest displays of self-righteousness he is saying, "How can someone like me who has done everything according to God's word have to suffer this great evil?" God's reply is for Job to shut up and listen.

How do you handle loss? How do you handle yourself when your world appears to be falling apart? What do you most people do, even Christians, when disaster strikes and it seems like all you have achieved in your life has been taken away from you permanently? Most, if not all people, and that includes Christians, experience distress, tribulations, and fear. Then, in your despair you begin to complain, sometimes bitterly. This is where the danger lies.

Because, as I said before, complaining can lead to you focus on the problem, and eventually to reject God. Satan knew this. This is why he (Satan) had Job's wife tell him (Job), "Must you maintain your integrity? Why don't you curse God and die." What frame of mind would you be in, if these unfortunate situations fall on you? Yes, you would be complaining and whining too. "Why me? Why me?" And of course some of your friends, associates, family, close relatives under the influence of Satan would be leading the charge to influence you to break from God. Complaining can lead to anger and sin, and can lead to 1) blaming God for your situation; 2) blaming God can lead to you removing yourself from God's will, and 3) may lead to imperfection.

How do we complain? "Why me, what did I do to deserve this? If God would just answer my prayers, give me a sign. Why does everything I do seem to go wrong? I wish I could turn the clock back I would change everything. Look at all the good that I have done, yet this happened to me. That was not right. I don't understand." Any of this sounds familiar?

Let us look Job's response to his situation. Job 10:1 states, *"I loathe my very life; therefore I will give free rein to my complaint and speak out in the bitterness of my soul."*

Job complains bitterly about his situation to the point of being self-righteous. Job is in a deep state of depression. Job is not handling this situation very well. In Job 1:20 he shaved his head; in Job 2:8 he sat in ashes; in Job 3 he deplores his birth; and in Job 6:8-13 he wants to die. Job 10:1-18 states *"Wherefore then hast thou brought me forth out of the womb?"* Job 17:1 says *"My spirit is broken;...."* And Job 19:25 states *"For I know that my redeemer liveth...."*

Sometimes in your complaint, as if to ease the pain a bit, you believe what has happened to you, was God's righteous judgment. Yet, God has not pass judgment on you. You read what happened to Job. You say things like; God knows what he is doing. He is always there for me. Job proclaims God's righteous judgment. The good news is that Job complains and whines, but does not turn his back on God. He stays firm footed in faith in God. Job 23:10 states, *"But he knoweth the way that I take: when he hath tried me, I shall come forth as gold."*

In your time of trials you may find all sorts of people are willing to give you advice. You must be careful as to what advice to take. You have to sift through all of it and purge out the bad and keep the good. Knowledge of the word of God helps you to do that. It must be the only measurement you use to determine what advice to take and what not to take. Your friends in particular are the ones to readily advise you. You must ask yourself, Are they believers? Do they have God's wisdom? Are they making spiritual sense? Or are they of the Devil sent to throw you off the path to perfection? Then you must be prepared to receive the advice and Godly counseling from that friend who has the spirit of God in him/her. Job found himself in such situation where his three friends have soundly criticized him. But now here comes Elihu with a different attitude, a welcome attitude.

What we are seeing in Elihu is evidence of Godly counseling. He is revealing the truth about God's ways to a distraught Job. Not by means of condemnation, but constructive Godly criticism that is not motivated by personal gain, but is an attempt to bring Job back to his senses, so to speak. This is kind of advice you must seek when is distress, and this is caliber of advisor you must seek out, or pray for. That friend whose intent is not to condemn, but to edify, remind, prod you in the direction of the Father's will. We all need an Elihu in your lives, a friend with the spirit of God in their hearts, a perfect friend to keep on the perfect path. (See Job Ch 32- 35). You must be patient in your trials and tribulations, and not be too hasty to cast judgment on God. Observe Elihu to Job in Job 34:5 -*9 "For Job hath said, I am righteous: and God hath taken away my judgment. 6) Should I lie against my right? my wound is incurable without transgression. 7) What man is like Job, who drinketh up scorning like water? 8) Which goeth in company with the workers of iniquity, and walketh with wicked men. 9) For he hath said, It profiteth a man nothing that he should delight himself with God."* In other words Elihu is saying, Job, watch what you say before God.

Notes

7

Strategies to Use in Times of Difficulties

Below are five strategies that you must adopt when dealing with your difficulties if you are to remain perfect.

1. God wants you to keep a cool head and be rational in your times of trials and tribulations

By not keeping a cool head you could easily be tempted by Satan to end your worship of God and serve other strange gods. You could be lead to do things that are sinful, and yield easily to ungodly advice from relatives and friends. When you become anxious you have a tendency to react, especially if your feet are not planted firmly in God's word. It becomes easy for you to want to "curse God and die." This is why some people turn to sin to solve their problems, but this only complicates the situation. This is why some people go as far as committing suicide. When you are faced with trials and tribulations, no matter how great or small they are, you must make every attempt to focus on God's wisdom, and do not ever question God's reasons for doing things. That is what Satan wants you to do. Always ignore advice from friends or family to do wrong, no matter how beneficial to you it may seem at the time. Remember, stay focused. Never react, for reactionary behavior is not of God. Observe part of God's reply to Job's complaining in Job 38:4, *"Where were you when I laid the foundations of the earth? Tell Me, if you have understanding."* You may read the rest of God's reply in Job 38.

2. **Watch the words that you speak, you may be condemning God and do not realize it. God is listening.**

You must be careful of not to condemn God when you are experiencing difficult times, when your plans have not fallen into place according to your timetable. You have not obtained the dream job, the wife or husband you prayed for has not materialized. Your financial situation has not improved in years, and the people who do not serve God, who do not care about God appear to be "prospering." That is when you start saying things like, "At this point in my life I should have accomplished this or that." Or things like, "God I trusted you, hoped in you, believed in you. I prayed and prayed and yet you have not answered me. Why me?" That is self-righteousness. Yes, and believe it or not, you have just judged God!

Observe God's response to Job: Job 40: 6-8 states, *"Then the LORD answered Job out of the whirlwind, and said: 7) Now prepare yourself like a man; I will question you, and you shall answer Me: 8) Would you indeed annul My judgment? Would you condemn me that you may be justified? 9) Have you an arm like God? Or can you thunder with a voice like His?"* NKJV. God is saying: Who are you to question my plans for you, Job? I know what I am doing. You need to chill and be still and know that I am God. You are not to question God's plan for your life. Just be patient and all will fall into the place. God loves you and will take care of you. Just trust Him to do what He knows is best for you. Trust Him to make you perfect.

3. Always be ready to humbly repent if you have said something against God's will

Job 40:4 gives Job's response to God, *"Behold, I am vile; what shall I answer thee? I will lay mine hand upon my mouth. 5) Once have I spoken; but I will not answer: yea, twice; but I will proceed no further."* Job responds to God in a manner that defines the word humble. It is as if he is saying, Yes God, you are right and I was wrong all along. I should have trusted you from the very beginning. I, whom you have blessed all my life, ought to know better than to think you will bring all these calamities on me and afflict me in this way. I should not have questioned your wisdom. "I am vile." I will be silent and still, and know that you are God. No wonder God said that Job was *perfect,* and upright, and feared God, and eschewed evil. You, too, must seek perfection!

As Christians you must have this same attitude of understanding and trust in God. Know that when things, good or bad, appear in your life that they are all ultimately for your good. If a dozen "bad" things happen to you and two good things happen to you, God will add those dozen negative things to your two good things and make them all good things. You see, they only appear as negative to you because you are looking at them with worldly eyes. Romans 8:28 states it clearly: *"And we know that all things work together for good to them that love God, to them who are the called according to his purpose."* Notice Paul says "we know". Ask yourself the questions, Do I really know this? And am I prepared to accept this? Do I believe this? If your answer is yes to all three questions, then you must be prepared to act on all three. Also Paul said "all things". All means all – the good, the bad, the ugly. You must never turn from this, never question God's will in your life. Just trust, trust, and trust! And be patient!!!

4. Be willing to seek forgiveness and praise God for His mercy and goodness which are forever

Job 42:2 states, *"I know that thou canst do every thing, and that no thought can be withheld from thee."* Job 42:6 says, *"Wherefore I abhor myself, and repent in dust and ashes."* When Job was confronted by God he was quick to admit the error of his ways and seek forgiveness. You must do the same when confronted by the Holy Spirit. When your pastor points out scriptures to you that convict you, there is no need to get angry at the pastor as some people do, just seize upon the moment to change from doing wrong to following God's will. Look at the pastor's convicting words as divine intervention from the Holy Spirit admonishing you to act appropriately. You must seek God's forgiveness. God is merciful and full of grace and will forgive you.

5. Finally, know that God will not only restore you, but will bless you even more

Observe Job 42:10: *"And the LORD turned the captivity of Job, when he prayed for his friends: also the LORD gave Job twice as much as he had before."* Is it not great that we serve a merciful God, a God that loves us, and is quick to forgive us no matter how ridiculous we may act? And not only forgives us, but blesses us in the process. Job 42:12-13: *"So the LORD blessed the latter end of Job more than his beginning: for he had fourteen thousand sheep, and six thousand camels, and a thousand yoke of oxen, and a thousand she asses. 13) He had also seven sons and three daughters."* All praise be to God.

Notes

8

How to Achieve Perfection

In order to achieve perfection, you *must* be willing to accept the teachings of the gospel. To begin with, you *must* be willing to listen to the word of God and *do* the word of God, and you must be willing to accept the fact that God's word (as stated in the Bible and *only* in the Bible) is the one and only true way of life – the only undeniable true reality. Observe these passages of scripture: Ephesians 4:11 - *"And he gave some, apostles; and some, prophets; and some, evangelists; and some, pastors and teachers; 12) For the perfecting of the saints, for the work of the ministry, for the edifying of the body of Christ:"*

There are those who have been anointed by God with the charge of edifying the saints in a way that leads to perfection. Are you willing to listen to those who have been given this special responsibility? You must be, in order to start on the road to perfection.

Matthew 7:24 states, *"Therefore whosoever heareth these sayings of mine, and doeth them, I will liken him unto a wise man (perfect man), which built his house upon a rock: 25) And the rain descended, and the floods came, and the winds blew, and beat upon that house; and it fell not; for it was founded upon a rock."* This man built a life that was perfect on a rock called the Word!

In Proverbs 24:13: *"My son, eat thou honey, because it is good; and the honeycomb, which is sweet to thy taste: 14) So shall the knowledge of wisdom be unto thy soul: when thou hast found it, then there shall be a reward, and thy expectation shall not be cut off."*

Matthew 5:48 says, *"Be ye therefore perfect, even as your Father which is in heaven is perfect."*

Matthew 5:44, 45 in a way present a strong case for seeking spiritual perfection. Matthew 5:44, *45 state, "But I say unto you, Love your enemies, bless them that curse you, do good to them that hate you, and pray for them which despitefully use you, and persecute you; 45) That ye may be the children of your Father which is in heaven (be perfect): for he maketh his sun to rise on the evil and on the good, and sendeth rain on the just and on the unjust."* This means that the sun and rain are not enough for perfection for the Kingdom, since the evil and unjust benefit from the sun and rain just as the just and unjust do. The sun and rain, in this context represent the ability to gather material things. In other words, physical (material) needs met do not mean perfection attained. There is a missing ingredient which is God's word.

If God gives sun and rain to the evil, and gives to the saints the same sun and rain then there must be more needed than the receiving of sun and rain in order for His saints to be perfect. In other words, your life is not perfect if you only rely on material things. You need the word of God to complete your life, to live that perfect life. To tell you the truth, this perfection has no basis in material gain, but is rooted in God's word. So you can live a perfect life whether you are experiencing a time of plenty or a time of little. Observe what Philippians 4:11,12 says, *"Not that I speak in respect of want: for I have learned, in whatsoever state I am, therewith to be content. I know both how to be abased, and I know how to abound: every where and in all things I am instructed both to be full and to be hungry, both to abound and to suffer need."* In other words, your spiritual state of being will not change no matter your circumstances. Now, that is the very essence of perfection that you must seek.

Paul is saying, no matter the circumstances I have the word of God to sustain me. This is not to say that you should not desire material things, but you should rather focus on God's word and have faith in God to provide you these things. Observe Deuteronomy 8:3: *"And he humbled thee, and suffered thee to hunger, and fed thee with manna, which thou knewest not, neither did thy fathers know; that he might make thee know that man doth not live by bread only, but by every word that proceedeth out of the mouth of the LORD doth man live."* This statement is repeated by Jesus when He was confronted by Satan. Matthew 4:4 states, *"But he (Jesus) answered and said, 'It is written, Man shall not live by bread alone, but by every word that proceedeth out of the mouth of God'."*

The Devil did not argue with Jesus, because he knew Jesus was right. So he changed the topic. He knew perfection and imperfection. The devil knows how to keep you in imperfection. Watch out when the

Devil is testing you through his agents (could be your trusted friends, family, close associates, etc.) who, when you prove them wrong, are always quick to change the topic to cause you to sin, to prove your imperfection. Satan tried that with Jesus three times in the wilderness. Jesus quoted God's word, indicating that He lives by God's word. He stood firm-footed in God's word. This must be your approach to life at all times if you are to gain this perfection that you seek. Notice, Jesus did not only say by *the* word that comes out of the mouth of God, but he said "but by *every* word..." (my italics). Every means all of God's word. What is an example of God's word? "Let there be light....) This light is the sun, the same sun that rises on the just and unjust. Even the unjust rely on God's word for their very existence. Their very existence is dependent on God's grace. They just do not know it nor accept it, and refuse to serve Him through thanksgiving and prayer. Ungrateful. Hence they continue to live in sin, in imperfection. As I said before, the sun and the rain provide for material things, but lack the spiritual things. This is where the word of God comes in, to help you through this evil world. This is how you can survive trials and tribulations. Observe Psalm 34:19, 20: *"Many are the afflictions of the righteous (the perfect): but the LORD delivereth him out of them all. 20) He keepeth all his bones: not one of them is broken."* How are you delivered, or how do you keep all your bones? By knowing and living according to the word of God. John 16:33 states, *"These things I have spoken unto you, that in me ye might have peace. In the world ye shall have tribulation: but be of good cheer; I have overcome the world."*

Remember, these key words of Jesus to Satan: "shall live". Shall live = bread and every word of God. Shall live does not simply mean being alive, but means the quality of life while you are alive. You can only achieve this higher standard through walking in obedience to God's word. This is how true prosperity comes. This is how the peace of mind comes. This is how you attain perfection. It is only by attaining perfection you are able to withstand these trials and tribulation Jesus speaks about.

The perfection you seek produces enormous benefits, such as peace of mind. That is, you must seek spiritual perfection because of the immeasurable benefits that spring forth from it. This includes the abundant, peaceful, satisfying life here on Earth and salvation in eternity.

Also, as a side note, the perfection that you seek must come from wisdom obtained from the Word of God, and not on one of those many talk shows that promote worldly wisdom. Remember, worldly wisdom is of Satan, and Satan comes "to steal, and to kill, and to destroy."

You must, therefore, engage in daily prayer to God through Jesus Christ, and also study the Bible every day. Obtaining an understanding of God through His word is a must do in the evil world in which you live. Go to church often. Do not fall for the belief that you can do it on your own. Hebrews 10:25 states, "*Not forsaking the assembling of ourselves together, as the manner of some* is; *but exhorting* one another: *and so much the more, as ye see the day approaching.*" 2 Timothy 2:15 states, *"Study to shew thyself approved unto God, a workman that needeth not to be ashamed, rightly dividing the word of truth."*

Notes

9

Scriptural References to Perfection

I leave you with these passages from the Bible:

Job 23:10-12: *"But he knoweth the way that I take: when he hath tried me, I shall come forth as (refined) gold (perfected). 11) My foot hath held his steps, his way have I kept, and not declined. 12) Neither have I gone back from the commandment of his lips; I have esteemed the words of his mouth more than my necessary food."*

James 1:2-4: *"My brethren, count it all joy when ye fall into divers temptations; 3) Knowing this, that the trying of your faith worketh patience. 4) But let patience have her perfect work, that ye may be perfect and entire, wanting nothing."*

John 17:23: *"I in them, and thou in me, that they may be made perfect in one; and that the world may know that thou hast sent me, and hast loved them, as thou hast loved me."*

Luke 6:40: *"The disciple is not above his master: but every one that is perfect shall be as his master."*

Proverbs 11:5: *"The righteousness of the perfect shall direct his way: but the wicked shall fall by his own wickedness."*

Psalm 18:32: *"It is God that girdeth me with strength, and maketh my way perfect."*

Psalm 37:37: *"Mark the perfect man, and behold the upright: for the end of that man is peace."*

Colossians 1:28: *"Whom we preach, warning every man, and teaching every man in all wisdom; that we may present every man perfect in Christ Jesus:"*

2 Timothy 3:16, 17: *"All scripture is given by inspiration of God, and is profitable for doctrine, for reproof, for correction, for instruction in righteousness: 17) That the man of God may be perfect, throughly furnished unto all good works."*

Hebrews 13:20, 21: *"Now the God of peace, that brought again from the dead our Lord Jesus, that great shepherd of the sheep, through the blood of the everlasting covenant, 21) Make you perfect in every good work to do his will, working in you that which is wellpleasing in his sight, through Jesus Christ; to whom be glory for ever and ever. Amen."*

1 Peter 5:10: *"But the God of all grace, who hath called us unto his eternal glory by Christ Jesus, after that ye have suffered a while, make you perfect, stablish, strengthen, settle you."*

Amen!

Jude 1:24, 25 *"Now unto him that is able to keep you from falling, and to present* you *faultless before the presence of his glory with exceeding joy, 25) To the only wise God our Saviour,* be *glory and majesty, dominion and power, both now and ever. Amen."*

Notes

About the Author

Bishop Allan Smith is the founder and pastor of New World Christian Center located in Houston, Texas. Pastor Smith has dedicated his life to teaching Biblical principles that serve to enhance the lives of believers. He has witnessed changes in the lives of those who embrace the Word of God through his dynamic and insightful teaching. Pastor Smith is of the firm belief that those who follow God's word will live a life of prosperity, the life that God promises to all who believe.

May God bless you.

Made in the USA
Charleston, SC
28 July 2010